We Both Speak English but...

by Heather Bradley

To my mum and her dad
without whom we
would not be cousins.

 FriesenPress

One Printers Way
Altona, MB R0G 0B0
Canada

www.friesenpress.com

ISBN
978-1-03-916961-6 (Hardcover)
978-1-03-916960-9 (Paperback)
978-1-03-916962-3 (eBook)

1. JUVENILE NONFICTION, PEOPLE & PLACES

Distributed to the trade by The Ingram Book Company

My cousin, Arlene says that I speak funny. She has an Irish accent like my mum. I tell her that she speaks *differently*. We both speak English but...

She takes the lift to the seventh floor.

I take the elevator.

She carries her lunch to school in a reusable cloth sack and her hot milk and sugar with tea in a flask.

I carry my lunch to school in a reusable cloth bag and my hot milk and sugar with tea in a Thermos bottle.

She has biscuits as a treat. I have cookies as a treat.

Arlene jumps rope
at break time.

I play skipping
at recess.

When it is rainy outside, she plays draughts.

When it is rainy outside, I play checkers.

When Arlene wants to splash in puddles, she wears a slicker and Wellingtons and carries a brolly.

When I go out to play in the rain, I wear a raincoat and rubber boots and carry an umbrella.

At school, Arlene plays
football on a team.

I play soccer on a team.

My cousin's mum puts groceries in the boot of her car.

My mum puts groceries in the trunk of her car.

Sometimes Arlene's mum sends her to the shoppe for a bap of bread.

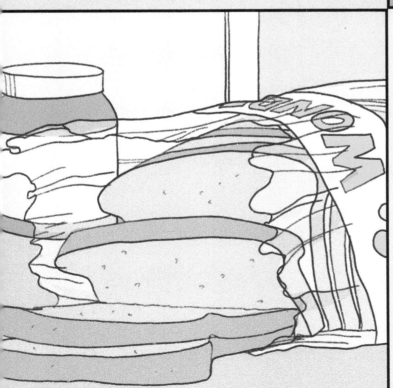

Sometimes my mum sends me to the store for a loaf of bread.

After school, Arlene eats a
pack of crisps while watching
a film on the telly.

I eat a bag of potato chips while I watch a movie on the TV.

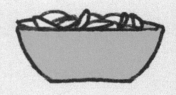

My cousin
wears trousers.

I wear pants.

She says that pants are underwear and wearing them in public is bonkers!

I say, "that is crazy!"

Sometimes Arlene
wears a frock.

I NEVER wear a dress unless my mum really wants me to.

Arlene keeps her clothes in a wardrobe.

I keep my clothes in the closet.

My cousin likes
striped stockings.

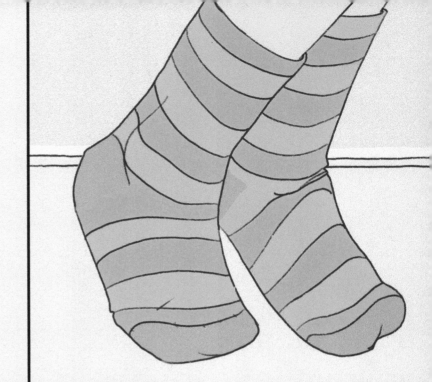

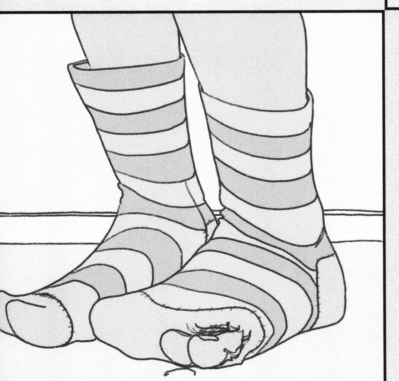

I like
striped socks.

When Arlene gets chilly, she puts on a jumper.

When I get cold, I put on a pullover.

Granny knit them both to match.

When Arlene hears
the chimes of the
ice-cream van, she gets
a poke and a flake.

When I hear the music
of the ice-cream truck,
I get a soft-serve ice-cream
cone but with no chocolate
bar sticking out of it.

My cousin says
"that's a cute wee dog"
even when it's a Great Dane!

I say wee when something
is teeny, tiny or small
like a ladybug.

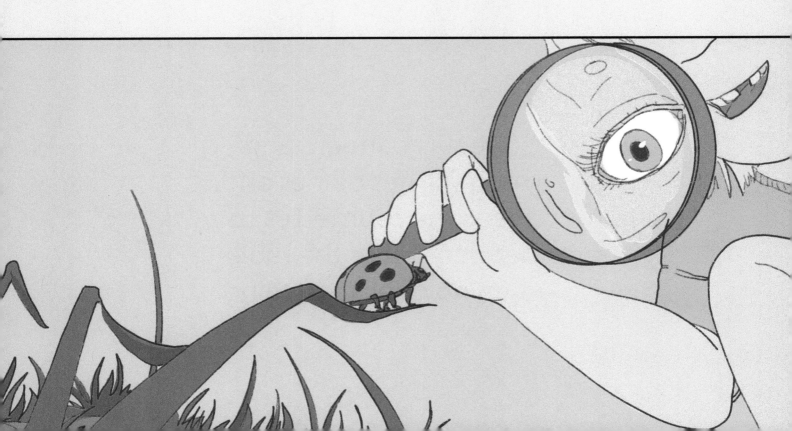

She has bangers and
mash for her dinner and
feeds the courgettes to
her dog under the table
when no one is watching.

I have sausages and mashed potatoes for my supper. I feed the zucchini to my dog under the table when no one is looking. I don't think Fluffy likes them either.

Arlene brushes her teeth in the loo.

She checks the looking glass to see if her misbehaving curl is laying across her forehead. It is.

I brush my teeth in the bathroom.

I check the mirror to see if my new front tooth has started to grow. It hasn't.

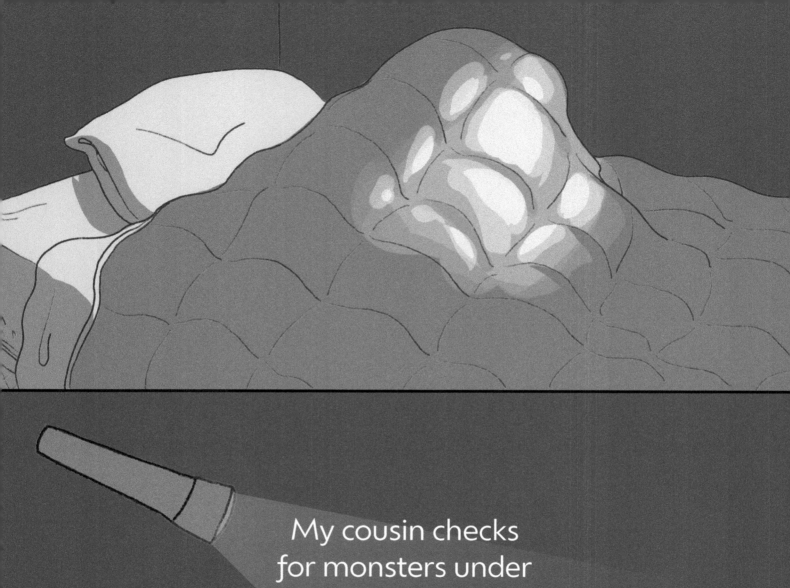

My cousin checks
for monsters under
her bed then reads
under the covers
with a torch.

I check for monsters
under the bed then
read under the covers
with a flashlight.

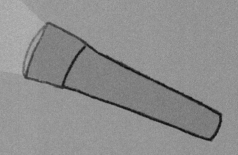

She calls her covers a duvet.

I call my covers a quilt.

Arlene says "Cheerio" when she leaves or stops talking on the telephone.

I giggle because it sounds like breakfast cereal.

I say bye, bye.

 Arlene dreams of
coming to Canada
to play with me and
to see Niagara Falls.

I dream of going to Ireland to play with Arlene and to see the Giant's Causeway and maybe ... a leprechaun!

Our words might be different,
but our hearts dream the same.
What we dream about the most is
doing all those things *together*.

Find ways that other people say the things you say.

I Say	They Say

9 781039 169616